ACTORS,
AUDIENCE,
AND THE STAGE

Also by Torry Fountinhead

The 7 Pillars Your Authentic Self Stands On
Part I of The Essential Companion Series

The Beauty, Part I of The Contemplation Series

The Soul's Openner – Enchanting The Soul to 'Being'
Part II of The Contemplation Series

Reach The Fountain of Youth
Part III of The Contemplation Series

You Are Allowed, Life Is A Gift
Part IV of The Contemplation Series

Shush! It's a Secret, The Lake Hides His Dummy
Part of The Rainbow of Life's Secrets

Life, The Amazing Story
Part of The Rainbow of Life's Secrets

Poem: Good Enough, Part of Forever Spoken, The International Library of Poetry

A Tip of an Iceberg Meditations, a series of short books among are:

Is Forgiving a Riddle?
Momentary Thoughts
The Life The Heart Sprouts
For As It Is The Mind That Makes The Body Rich
Unveil From All The Coats, Sing Your Heart

and many more at work…

Actors, Audience, and The Stage

Part VI of "A Tip of an Iceberg Meditations"
Series

By

Torry Fountinhead

Airé Libré Publishing & Computing Ltd.

eBook ISBNs:
ISBN-10: 0-9733450-1-2
ISBN-13: 978-0- 9733450-1-8

Print Book ISBNs:
ISBN-10: 0-9733450-2-0
ISBN-13: 978-0-9733450-2-5

© 2018 Torry Fountinhead
All Rights of this work are Reserved.   No part or whole may be used, copied or reproduced, stored in retrieval systems, or transmitted, in any form or by any means whatsoever, including electronic media, mechanical, photocopying, recording, or otherwise.

For more information contact:
Airé Libré Publishing & Computing Ltd.
Suite 306, 185-911 Yates St.
Victoria BC V8V 4Y9 Canada
Tel: 1-250-592-3099.
http://www.al.bc.ca   info@al.bc.ca

Book Web-Site URLs:
http://actorsaudienceandthestage.atipofanicebergmeditations.ca

Part of:
Http://www.atipofanicebergmeditations.ca
Http://www.tipofaniceberg.ca
Http://www.atipofanicebergmeditations.com
Http://www.tipofaniceberg.com

I dedicate this book to all of us, those who like the part they are playing, and those who do not.

"Denying your Authentic Self significance, and taking on false identities, is like denying your existence."

Torry Fountinhead

vi

Table of Content

Actors, Audience, and The Stage	i
Also by Torry Fountinhead	ii
Actors, Audience, and The Stage	iii
Copyrights	iv
Dedication	v
Table of Content	vii
Actors, Audience, and The Stage	ix
Part One	1
Prologue	3
Chapter I The Show	5
Chapter II A Specific Stage	11
Chapter III When You Are A Player	17
Chapter IV Which One to Be When	21
Chapter V Another Layer of 'Being'	25
Chapter VI Images and Flowing As	29
Chapter VII The Flowing or Written Destiny	33
Chapter VIII The Play of A Life	37
Chapter IX Being Authentically You	41
Chapter X The Tapestry brush-strokes & Consciousness	45
Epilogue	49
Part Two	53
A Thought Put To Paper	55-98
A word about this series	99

Actors, Audience, and The Stage

Actors, Audience, and The Stage

Part One

Actors, Audience, and The Stage

Prologue

William Shakespeare Stated (and mused) in *Jaques* speech from *As You Like It* that:

> *"All the world's a stage,*
> *And all the men and women merely*
> *players; They have their exits and their*
> *entrances; And one man in his time*
> *plays many parts…"*

He was not that far off from King Solomon's view of people and Life, or what we actually find in Life.

Let us *set the stage* for this book, so we may both be able to follow the line-of-thought that states that all life is an illusion, all is just a phantom, and see if it is actually so.

You might ask, what do I mean by the 'line-of-thought,' to which I will answer in some ways throughout the book, and here I will just say:

Is it not a wonder that for thousands of years many cultures weaved stories, belief systems, religions, fables, fairy tales, and what not, to describe what is Life, and yet, they always pound on us the importance of being 'attached' to The Reality.

What is the Reality, and is there only one unique one.

How many times did I hear people reflect on other people: "they live in their own world, their own reality, but never in the true reality?!"

What if the actual stage is the Reality, but what is being played on it, and its perception, is the phantom?

So let us dive in, for a while, and contemplate it, there is much more to say.

Chapter I
The Show

"Hello There!" said the usher, "your seat is right here. Enjoy the show."

You have found yourself in a strange theatre, not in an auditorium, or a closed facility, but out and about, in the middle of town.

Well, is that not grand? The seat was on a single bench, surrounded by green grass, right under beautiful blue skies, strewn with wispy feathered white clouds, helping reduce the baking of the hot sun; There was no movement, but for a light breeze that even left the tree leaves at a motionless peace.

It felt so strange, but look, you saw a stationary dog, as if waiting, and as soon as you looked at it, the dog started to wag its tail and bark, short, attention requesting, barks.

You looked aside, and saw a young tall slim man – he only shown signs of life at the point of time that you have acknowledged his existence, but what was he doing just standing there?

Looking further on, you found a young lady running, motionless in mid-stride, head looking back at the young man, and again, as soon as you have perceived her, she was back into her run, waving the young man Goodbye.

What was that all about?

How could it be?

What is the story?

You leaned back into the bench, deep in thought, deciding to take in the whole panorama versus just a segment of it.

The street came alive, as you looked more, and more, into the details of it.

Traffic was about, double-decker buses, yellow and blue taxies, even horse and carriage on a tour of the city. People were standing looking into shops' windows, admiring the quaint merchandise. There were cyclists weaving their way between the cars, sometimes jumping onto the pavement to save time, and back onto the street, ahead of all other cars.

The street, in itself, was quite beautiful. Flowering hanging baskets hung from each light post, and larger pot plants were on each street corner; The pavement was actually made of cut-stone, and immaculately clean; For a change, there was no diesel powered vehicle to spoil the scenery with its smell.

Over to one side, you noticed a street guitar player, strumming his guitar in a haunting wonderful rhythm, humming to himself in the process. He was so engrossed in his music that it seemed as if he occupied a separate world of his own.

There was much more to see, but suddenly you felt the strain, and closed your eyes – what was that? You could hear nothing. In an alarming feeling, you opened your eyes, only to discover that all was standing still again, and only once you really looked at it – it all came to life and movement again.

How strange!

You still could not understand what was this show about, what was the story – if any, and what were you doing here watching it.

A moment later, the usher was at your side, smiling and beckoning you to come. Where to?

In the instant that you stood up and took your first step, the usher disappeared while, the scenery returned to movement, and life; Only at this time, you were part of it, and regardless where you looked, all was in motion, even the resting guitar player shown his breathing rhythm, and smiled.

In one moment, you became part of the scenery, now, as turning from an observer to a participator, you have felt, you could decipher the story of this show.

Immediately though, you had a question forming in your mind, 'how could it be that I came in as an observer, and thereafter, became a participator?'

How could it be that when you were an

observer, while you closed your eyes, all stood still, and as soon as you have opened your eye, all became alive again?

Now, inside the show, you tested it, and closed your eyes, but strange – you could hear the activity, and even feel it – nothing stood still, even the tree leaves were moving in the breeze now.

What was the key to this show?

Actors, Audience, and The Stage

Chapter II
A Specific Stage

The green grass still called you to rest, so you took off your sandals, and set on the grass, burying you toes in its cool velvety feel.

It felt like real grass, real ground, real air, and real people, so what was this specific stage?

At that moment, I passed you by, and you have called to me, 'excuse me, may I have a moment of your time?'

Yes, I answered, I have been waiting for

you.

'You have?!'

Well, yes, you see, when a person is awoken from Life's stupor, we are always there. You have just awoken.

I am sure you have many questions, and even more to come, but let us start from the fundamentals, and build your tower of understanding, as it were, on a solid ground. Mind you, nothing is solid, but for the sake of easy reference, we will use that phrase.

The first, and most important key, is understanding consciousness. There are many layers to it, as well as tiers.

When you visit a hospital, and see unconscious people, you may question if they are still alive; The doctors and nurses will say, well, their hearts and bodies are still functioning, even if sometimes aided by machines, so yes, they are still alive, but their mind is not active.

This is what they believe!

If you will watch a sleeping person, you would think that he, too, seems unconscious. Is he?

You may continue to look at different levels of activity, of a living person, thinking that it may denote their level of consciousness, but here lies the key.

The key is in the actual word.

To Human Beings, the word consciousness denotes the mind activity of a living person. Thus, when you are asleep, you are not counted as conscious, and so forth. In truth, the word consciousness has a dual meaning, the one – that the person is in contact with their mind, and the second – that they are awake, and aware.

Take for example that guitar player, sitting at the street corner, but hardly noticing the passers-by, when he is engaged deeply in his melody.

He is active, so people assume he is conscious. He is playing his guitar, and I might add – beautifully, so he must be conscious, otherwise, how would he even be able to carry the melody on the strings. He smiles at the strangers who watch him while, he is humming the tune. When he will finish for the day, he will collect the money given to him, pack his guitar, and head on his way.

Yet, is he awake? Is he aware of the Life he lives in?

Only if we will talk to him, and ascertain his views, we might know.

While Human Beings consider that a person is conscious if active, the Universe and All-That-Is consider conscious one who is connected to their own mind *and* the Universal Mind – one who is aware of the play of Life, and of Life itself.

You see, Life within the Universal Mind is the stage, upon which numerous number of plays are played simultaneously; Some seen, and some unseen.

Are you familiar with the concept of dimensions?

Like the multiple layers of an onion, layers of dimensions are laid upon Creation, but unlike an onion, the layers are not separated – they intertwine.

In each Dimension, there are defined beings, forms, creative forces, and laws, none of which affect another dimension unless, acting within the other dimension's laws of creation.

In this dimension, of your own world, you mostly see that which appears in three-dimensional form, feel that which you open yourself to feel although, you might feel unseen things, but not give them a name, or sometimes even – attention.

You might also sense much more, but only when you will develop your awareness, will you be able to relate to that.

Consciousness with awareness is very much like an iceberg. The wind that affects the tip of it will transmit information to the bottom of it while, it may also be affected by a strong undercurrent of the sea.

Animal, who senses danger, will flee to a higher ground. Human Beings, on the other hand, will stay put and fight, but not necessarily save themselves, or the day.

Therefore, let us divide things in the manner of which they are being perceived. Let us say that physical things are both seen and physically felt, if touched. Feelings are perceived either as emotions, or sensations; Some are known, and some are nameless. In addition to it, there are sensed sensations that are so subtle that they are sublime, and therefore, beyond Human comprehension.

Some Dimensions have a sensation affect onto other dimensions, but never override any specific dimensional activity.

The stage, therefore, is like the basis of the

tapestry, the weaved-cloth that the tapestry will be embroidered upon, with multiple colours, and themes.

I would also like to add that the whole of Creation is the main tapestry while, each dimension becomes its own tapestry – a tapestry-section that only comprises a specific main theme.

Chapter III
When You Are A Player

Remember when you took the first step, and all came alive, and remained alive, even though you closed your eyes?

This was the moment you became part of the story, the Life, within that show; By being conscious of yourself, and the others, you tacitly agreed to affect them, and be affected by them in return.

When one is part of the story, knowingly or

unknowingly, They have an effect on others; This is why one should be called to acknowledge their responsibility.

Let me talk, for a moment, about a basic rule of Creation. Creation is caused by Love – the wish to give it and thus, eventually also to received it.

Each form in existence, whether seen or not, is a vessel, in which streams of Love and Beauty are streaming into and through it. The vessels are created pure and 'good', with no blemish whatsoever. They are also fully capable of receiving, and allowing through, unrestricted and boundless amount of Love and Beauty. There are no two forms – vessels, which are equal in form, but all are equal in capability.

Life in Creation is not really a choice, which is made by any particular vessel, as it is described by the artist who created the tapestry's theme.

The tapestry's theme calls for experiences to become the 'brush strokes', the yarn and the stitches to paint it forth. The story then is told by the stitches, as they draw the picture upon the tapestry.

Actors, Audience, and The Stage

We defined the tapestry, as the stage, upon where the play is taking place. We also defined that the main play comprises a multitude of simultaneously played smaller, more personal, plays.

It is quite wonderful to stand afar and look at the beautiful tapestry alas, while you are a player, the full picture might escape your notice. Therefore, it is here that you, as one of the vessels, can, and will benefit from, using the gift of alternating between the positions of participator, and observer; Let us call these roles: the player, and the audience.

Actors, Audience, and The Stage

Chapter IV
Which One To Be When

Before we are going to look at the 'play', let us look at the vessel that a Human Being is.

For the sake of re-instating something of great importance, let me repeat myself and say: *"Each form in existence, whether seen or not, is a vessel, in which streams of Love and Beauty are streaming into and through it. The vessels are created pure and 'good', with no blemish whatsoever. They are also fully capable of receiving, and allowing through, unrestricted and boundless amount of Love and Beauty. There are no two forms – vessels, which are equal in form, but all are equal in capability";* It is the fundamental bouncing-board for greatness that each vessel has from its creation.

This will bring the important understanding that receiving and giving is a natural state of each vessel. Each vessel also is endowed with number of other innate gifts, sometimes working for it, and sometimes against it.

Remember that the vessel is more like a 'pipe' than a closed vessel. This is a key point, on which Human Beings, with their forgetfulness, seem to trip over, time and time again, feeling and thinking that all is limited; This problem stems from the sudden realisation that they are actually separate in their form from all others.

The separateness of forms does not mean, and does not denote on any limit (whatsoever) in the supply of Love and Beauty. The vessels are centres of action, like swirling spheres of light, in a constant movement. In addition, the Love and Beauty, streaming forth to each vessel, are pure and unconditional – with no agenda, blemish, or judgement.

Reading the scriptures, or any other literature that exist today, might give you the impression that judgement is part of *All*, but this is a false impression.

Remembering that the vessel is a vessel, looking at oneself sometimes from within the play, and sometimes only observing it, allows the vessel – Human Being, to gain a better understanding about himself; The idiom: *'Know Thy Self'* is not a cliché.

When the question is asked: *Which One To Be When*, one must understand that a constant flow between the two states will be for the best benefit. Like a dancer does not ask 'if' to take the next step, so the Human Being should 'flow' with the rhythm of necessity.

A clue may be that if you feel overwhelmed, confused, have an unanswered question, in puzzlement, or amazement, this is a call to change states – from player to observer; Allow yourself to change perception, by changing your vantage point, and thus, your open yourself to a better understanding.

Remember that flowing between both states, the player and participator, does not retract from your ability to live Life to the fullest, it actually allows you to choreograph a new type of dance – driven by interest and joy, and gives you enough pauses to exercise your power of choice.

Chapter V
Another Layer of 'Being'

For the sake of simplicity, let us identify two main layers of 'Being'. The one, is being in either the state of a *participator – Actor*, or *observer – Audience*. The second, calls for using different facets of yourself.

Life is a flowing dance, each step takes you to another experience and thus, requires of you to 'be' different in some way. You are like a beautifully polished diamond of many facets, shining the light in multiple hues. The whole diamond is you;

There is no separation of one facet from another, or the whole diamond, as they are all of the one diamond. Imagine that each experience draws from you a different image of yourself and thus, you show yourself to be versatile, and adaptive.

Each one of those facets may also be used in the many 'roles; that a person plays, both in different plays, and within the same play.

An important point to be stressed here is that the situations – the dance steps – require of you to make use of your power of choice – your free will. You are to act for your highest good, without harming any other person, or being, and therefore, you may choose that facet of you, which will serve you best. For example, being quick to react, may save someone's life while, being poised and polite, may save a situation, or a relationship.

Your mind swirling, you interrupted, and asked: "but how would I look to others, they will think I am just like a chameleon, and might even think that I am unstable?"

I sighed a sigh of sorrow, and answered your expecting face.

This requires a small sidetrack to let you know of a grave misunderstanding on behalf of

Humanity.

You see, Human Beings are not, and do not have the role, of a rock's solidity. True, Human Beings prefer to have a person acting in a structured and known manner – no surprise, because then they, themselves, can be less challenged, saved from the requirement of original thought, and adaptation.

Somewhere, the misunderstanding that being 'in the flow' meant being on a constant move, and it must be forward, was born in the minds of people, but it is so untrue, and far away from the real way of Life.

When a flower unfolds from a day old bud to a full bloom, you do not blame it that it is not something else, or even a different flower. You accept its stages as natural, because they are. Think of yourself, as that flower, with a single difference that you may choose to forever stream from bud to full bloom, back to bud, again, and again, as many times you wish, for the rest of your life.

If a person is tired, and needs to go to sleep, surely you do not expect them to get up and run a marathon – just because someone else you know might do it, at that same hour. That person is still the same dear one you know only, they happen to be tired – this is displaying one minute facet, which might be undesirable, but true.

Therefore, coming back to the need of having, and utilizing, another layer of being, would actually show you that it is required of you to acknowledge that you have at your disposal the ability, and realization, that you are of many facets, and allowed to call upon the one that is the Right one for the moment.

Remember, you only live one moment at a time!

Chapter VI
Images and Flowing As

Let us have a look at the 'stitches' that our tapestry comprises.

The stitches paint an 'image' similar to your experience with a photograph taken with a camera. The photograph, once taken, represents one specific moment in time, and your expression in it. For example, if you were listening to a joke being told, and then burst into laughter, and were photographed at the moment of laughter, the picture can only convey the fact that you had a laugh, but not the preceding moments of listening with a straight face.

You were afraid to be imagined as changeable as a chameleon, but if you study it closely, the chameleon's choice to blend with its environment, for either safety, or display of a certain state, shows how stable it is rooted in the present moment, and his reality.

Similarly, the multi-faceted shining diamond, with its continuous shining of rainbow-wide colours, does not denote instability, it only denotes variability while, remaining true to itself.

Think of each image, as an experience, and of yourself, as donating your experiences to a pool of wisdom and storytelling.

Do you really expect yourself to have the same expression throughout your life? How would we then distinguish you from an old-fashion robot?

Even if you observe yourself in the mirror, and follow your breath, you will see many changes of expression, whether they would be large or minute, occurring as you breathe.

You are a 'moveable', 'expressionist', and 'alive' creature; surely you cannot deny that – could you? This is true, of course, while you are aware in your own reality.

Your tapestry-section therefore, includes multitude of expressions of every moment of your life, in each stitch, expressing the 'story' of your life.

You can imagine then how complex is the tapestry, as a whole.

I could show you a multi-layered scarf, in which each side of it, the top-side and the under-side, both depict beautifully, as if either one is the top-side, but with a different colour scheme. If you were to be asked, which one is the topside, you could not have answered unless, you would voice an opinion to which colour you prefer at that specific moment.

Creation's tapestry, and all of its sections therein, is a complex form of a similar weave, stitching, and portraying of all dimensions, experiences, stories, and wisdom in existence, whether seen, or unseen.

It is because Human-Beings concentrate so much on the physicality, as it appears in the third-dimension, that they ignore the possibility of a complex, multi-layered existence, in which they may be active, and alive.

Your consciousness is supremely faster than

your best awareness, and certainly faster than your perception ability. Therefore, with all due respect, you cannot attest fully to your living experiences.

This is where flow state is so important. When in flow, you apply less judgment and therefore, less restriction upon yourself, and others. Unlike a detective who requires all facts in order to build up the crime picture, you are a Life-Dancer who *trusts* in the movement of Life, because you are a witness to it, every day of your life.

You are familiar with your day-and-age films, knowing that in actuality it is a flow of singular picture slides, which form the movement on the screen, versus the film being a multi-dimensional moving hologram. Your life, on the other hand, is not a conglomeration of slides. Your Life is a multi-dimensional hologram in endless movement – in flow.

Your breathing proves it.

You innate knowing of it, allows your trust to exist, whether you acknowledge it, or not.

It is part of your innate growth-ability.

Chapter VII
The Flowing or Written Destiny

Bearing in mind the previous example of a film, and the existence of a main theme, as I have stated before, we need to make some points a little clearer here.

The main theme of creation is the flowing of Love – the giving and receiving of it, which sustains Creation as a whole. See this theme as the underlining of all other themes and thus, it influences them.

Each dimension in Creation has also their own theme. In your own life on Earth, you are part of a specific theme. Your own life has its own theme as well. Therefore, the same complexity of tapestries, as referred to earlier, exists also in the themes.

A film, in contrast, once filmed, and put on the media that carries it, is done, and every time you will watch it, the same story will unfold before you, unlike the unfolding of a Human life.

It is important to distinguish between a theme and a destiny. Some religions will say that the Human destiny, and the celestial bodies destiny is written and sealed, but it is not so.

In Creation, and in each part of it from the smallest to the largest, all is in a state of growth, and thus, flows endlessly.

The destiny of each form, may it be Human, celestial, or any other type, is driven by the form's life theme, but a person, for instance, may interpret the theme in many ways.

Similar to a story that has a theme, a plot, characters, scenes, and experiences of all sorts, the life of a person would have them all, and more.

Furthermore, the personality traits, likes

and dislikes, belief systems, prejudices, moods, whims, reactions, wishes, desires, fears, and many more things, will influence how that person's story will unfold.

Unless, the person will become aware, and will endeavour to mould their life, like the potter moulds the clay.

The difference between applying awareness, and not, is the same as between living a 'prescribed' life to a 'creative' life.

A prescribed life will always follow accepted expectations, toeing the line sort of speak, while, a creative life will always spring forth from the culmination of the given states, and options of the moment.

People could consent to alter their words definition, instead of defining destiny as a given history, to define it as a theme driven – free flowing life story. Envisaging a state of choice where, the theme of your life may inspire you to choose a better momentary action and thus, moulding your future – and your destiny.

When you arrive at a feeling that you do not have a choice, and have to toe the line, ask why are you in that situation, and if you want to carry on being in it. Every action has a benefit associated with it, the question is if the benefit outweigh the disadvantages.

Sometimes, re-framing the parts that make up the situation's definition in your mind, and rearranging them, will alter your perception of the situation, and your reaction to it. Once you see it differently, you may choose your most graceful exit point.

You can see how being aware, responsible to your own being and life, striving to live your life's theme as best you can, while, acknowledging the dance of life, is a definition of a creative life, full of freedom.

Chapter VIII
The Play of A Life

Imagine the following, an entity of all goodness, love, compassion, and beauty decides to 'take-on' a life. At first step, the entity chooses the theme according to some visions and requirements, and secondly, it finds where best it could 'live' this theme – mostly.

The 'taking on' life action manifests as a conception of a foetus, and this is the start – the first step taken 'in life'; From here on, the entity either immerse itself entirely in this 'role', acts it out, as the actor, or chooses to alternate between the two states of actor and audience, by sometimes playing the 'role', and sometimes 'de-rolling' from it.

The 'play of a life,' in actuality, encompasses the main theme of that life, and there are many sub-plays, as per the sub-roles the entity plays.

I just mentioned that the entity might choose to either play the role in an engrossed manner, or alternate between participator and observer; There are at least two defining conditions that may cause the entity to make that choice.

The first, when all is well and loving, the messages received from its physical senses may be intoxicating; This sensual input is so joyful that the entity would like to immerse in it entirely, and even small interruptions will not dissuade it from remembering only the joy.

The second, alas, is when some form of harm is inflicted on the foetus, or child, that in response to the survival mechanism instilled in us, the entity will choose to fragment out, for a short and/or long periods of time. This harm is measured by the entity's capability to 'bear' the load of what is being inflicted , at that time. Therefore, you might find these entities switching on and off between the two states, as in a first defence mechanism.

There is nothing wrong with alternating the two states, it is though advisable to maintain a healthy connection, and measure of the two points of view.

It is interesting that Human Beings are only assured while identifying with their physical part, but we first, and foremost, a spirit entity using a physical apparatus to live in the third-dimensional time/space reality. Hence, it is all right to choose to be in either one of the two states, actor or audience, participator or observer, as long as we remember our current 'play'.

In our current 'play', we have created an identity, which we identify with. For example, the role of a mother is very precise; She is the mother of a specific child, so when she fetches the child from kindergarten, or school, she know which one to fetch. This is driven by the explicit identity associated with her role as mother.

For the same token, your place of home, work, friends, bank, town, country, and so on, is all associated with the identity you assume, and operate with.

Your main play is informed by the theme

the your entity chose for this lifetime. Whereby, within this 'lifetime', your many choices create many more sub-plays, and sub-roles. You might be a woman who is also a wife and mother, or you might be a single woman instead. You might have a profession further to being a home maker, and thus have a different role at your professional arena.

If you have performed an act of kindness – you might even appear as a saving angle to someone.

We tend to take it for granted, but here is where I would like you to remember my analogy of the diamond and the facets. You are the whole diamond, who happens to have multiple facets, shining and refracting the light differently, as you look at each facet.

Maturity of character therefore, is the measure of how well you recognise this, and how well you are able to flow from facet to facet, maintaining the coherency of your own main identity.

Chapter IX
Being Authentically You

Do you remember that awhile back we spoke of your fear to appear as changeable? Like a chameleon?

Well, I will remind you again of your 'Diamond Being'. Being the diamond – you are being authentically true to yourself. An extreme example would be that if one of your 'core values' is the preciousness of life, you would not go about killing people, whim-fully.

Yes, there are people and nations that choose to kill people for what seems to them to be a necessity, but in truthfulness, they have a problem that they do not seem to find a solution for, and they cannot bear the thought of remaining in that particular situation. Needless to say, that some belief systems will also play a major part in their decision.

Let us go back to the personal level, because it is the root of all understanding; It is the wisdom gained on an individual level that informs the whole of Humanity, as well as Creation. It is the emotional reacting, or pro-acting that will determine the hues that colour the individual's belief systems.

Norms, and belief systems, are created from the individual level to the national, and global, levels, and not the other way around. You may ask, why there are so many negative ones, to which I will answer that as many moment of time there are in a life of a person – such there are opportunities to cement a norm, or a belief system.

You see, reactions trigger either fear or appreciation, which create an emotional response that registers within every cell of your being; There on, informing all your future deductions, as they will be used as yardsticks for your own measuring of a situation.

A child that might witness another adult in pain, almost automatically will register fear even if it feels compassion, the main reason being understanding; The child might not have the faculties and knowledge to understand the cause for that pain specifically, if the cause is internal.

At the same time, the child will develop a like, or dislike, to such an appearance that will inform his reactions for the rest of his life. Furthermore, if the adult, now indisposed, cannot serve the child's needs, at that specific time, the child will develop an opinion along the line 'they were not there for me when I needed them'; Alas, the adult might have been there at any other time, but people seem to hold onto bad memories tighter than to good ones.

This is why I am using the analogy of the diamond; You are not fallen leaves of a tree blown by the wind, as the situations of your life occur; You are a stable One Being who has multiple facets, roles, and plays, but with the one main play at its core.

An actor, on the stage, might appear in many plays throughout their life, and it does not matter what 'persona' the actor takes in each of those plays, in actuality, when the curtain falls, the actor is back to the level of an individual person; When the actor sleeps, eats, brushes teeth, or any other acknowledged personal activity – the person is one – the One Diamond.

Furthermore, that same actor may use information gained at one play, to be re-used in another play, all of which are the plays this actor chooses to play.

Maybe another analogy may illustrate this situation in a more favourable light to you; When you, the one person, reads multiple books, at different times, neither the books or the times are the same; The only equal part in them, is you – the reader.

Each book can take you to a different surrounding – as the story goes, but you – the person – do not change, only the usage and location of your consciousness does.

Your consciousness usage and location, and the story weaved in that moment of life will create emotional responses within your being, which, yet again, will inform the whole of your being, Humanity, and Creation.

Chapter X
The Tapestry brush-strokes & Consciousness

Let you and I, while strolling on the promenade watching the passers-by, try to look at the whole scenery in a n encompassing manner.

Remember the core theme of Life being the main stage of Creation, and therefore – the main tapestry; That which you are witnessing here, in this third dimension life, is but a portion of what is happening; Nevertheless, each person, animal, plant, or even a rock that you see has the hidden factor, which is their main theme of life.

Their actions and expressions, that you are witnessing right now, are but a facet of their being shown to you momentarily.

The guitar player is an excellent example; He is playing and humming – at this moment, you might even imagine that at the same time he is thinking of a beloved one, or of a composition, or even if he would have enough money to buy dinner, from this day's efforts.

Yet, the guitar player does not share with you all of this, and you are only witnessing this one facet he chose for you to see.

Any person, on this street, has more roles they play in one play, and more plays in a life time that you would know of, or even if they are aware of.

If I am to ask you who and what you are, how many details do you think your answer will include?

It is this that will make a difference to the brush-strokes stitched upon the tapestry, both the main one of Life, and the personal sub-tapestry.

One person, may be a man who is a son, father, uncle, nephew, husband, dancer, singer, craft maker, employee, boss, entrepreneur, a property owner, a member of a club, a marathon runner, and so much more; These are just examples, but each one is a facet of the One Diamond that that man is, and has a full range of activities, all creating a specific reality of this facet.

All that I have mentioned is just noticeable in the physical reality of the third dimension, but understand that it is just a fraction of all that is happening, at the same time.

If you will proceed in granting every emotion, action ,reaction, and activity, a specific colour, and shade of colour, you could have just a mere glimpse of how intricate the Human tapestry is.

This is why it is a good exercise to step out – de-role, and become the observer – audience of your own life; It is certainly a good way to check yourself out whether, you weave a life-story and a theme, which is authentic to your life's theme, as well as one you can appreciate.

Here is where consciousness, and your awareness of it, is at its most importance; Your consciousness changes location and context according to what your attention is focused on, and your actual condition and activity.

I love imagining consciousness like the wind; The wind caresses all that it passes, it touches upon all with no judgement, or preference – it is in its true dance.

That that you are is like the wind; Your Spirit floats upon life with the same non-attachment, while in total acknowledgement of its being; Alas, when you 'come down to earth', (with a small e), your Spirit is then fully aware of your physical manifestations, including your own body, and is restricted in its free flow.

Your consciousness is not depended on your body, whilst your body is inter-depended on your consciousness; This also the reason you are active in other dimensions at the same time, as well as having full and engaging experiences while asleep.

The tapestry's brush-strokes embroider a fascinating intricate picture, full of magnificent experiences' records in colour; The consciousness of everything in Creation contributes to it- none excluded.

Epilogue

You looked at me with a mischievous smile, and said – "so it is as if God the Creator commissioned a huge wall-hanging tapestry to be made, and uses all experiences experienced in Creation as its brush-stroke, correct?

If so, is that the reason that everything in Creation has a consciousness, so everything will have the ability to experience?"

I smiled at you proudly, knowing that you have understood the gist of things.

It is always a pleasure to see an understanding turning to an applied wisdom – I responded.

You responded with a warm glowing face, and continued to comment – "so this is why it is better to have joyful experiences, because an experience turned to a brush-stroke has no preference if it is suffering, or joy."

I would like to highlight to you that although you are correct in this assumption, the reason why the joy path is preferable is that it is easier for any consciousness to evolve and grow via joy than via suffering, as joy is a natural encourager.

If you would look around you carefully, you may be able to see the glowing light of consciousness within everything, and its appearance just as an overcoat. Thus, you will realise that all is about performing the first, and foremost, act of Awareness.

This is why I have said earlier that *life is like a flowing dance*, and all in Creation are dancing with it.

Now, it is of outmost importance that you, and others, will take a step back, from Actor to Audience, from participator to observer, and see your arenas of playing, your methods of appearance, your actions and reactions, and your relationship to all of these.

When you have found yourself in what you referred to as a strange theatre, you actually arrived at it after evolving to a great degree by yourself; A moment of rest – was all it took to actually activate your inner knowing, and snap you to a larger reality, because your consciousness already has expended to its direction.

You, and I, were talking tacitly from your conception; We are talking personally now, because of your readiness, and your receptivity. Your evolution was, and is, ongoing from the moment of your creation, as a particular consciousness – and not only since you started to expose yourself to some metaphysical material , or teachings of others.

Everything, and everyone, has the innate ability to evolve; It is easier for the inanimate objects, planets, plant kingdom, and animals to proceed with it gracefully, as they do not allow their form of mind to distract them so much.

Human Beings on the other hand, are distracted very easily, because they allow their emotions to get in the way; They also indulge in developing opinions, prejudices, belief systems, and fears, all of which are non-required obstacles.

Although you have reached such a degree of evolution, I would suggest that you would carry on with the self-investigation, aimed at a better know-thy-self state, because Creation is evolving – and you are within it.

Suddenly, you said that your mind is racing with investigative questions, assessing one's situation, and you would like to write them down; I could see that 'talking' ceased to be of value, at that moment, so lovingly, I bid you farewell, and a promise that we will meet again.

The usher reappeared, and so did the bench, it had an embroidered notebook on it with a quill and ink; You looked surprised, but the usher just nodded approval, and led you to it.

You took it as a sign to go ahead, and make use of it all, and decided to declare it as your *'Resting Inspired Bench',* and from then on, it became your own.

The usher disappeared, peace and tranquillity were all around you, despite all the activity of the scene, and you commenced to put pen to paper.

Actors, Audience, and The Stage

Part Two

Actors, Audience, and The Stage

A Thought Put To Paper

In this second part of the book, I would like to present you with an opportunity to get to know yourself better, no probing, just a private *"for your eyes only"* look at YOU.

The idea is to remain light-hearted and adopt a joyful way to look at yourself, in the manner a loving parent might look at their toddler child, and how they discover the world around them – lovingly, compassionately, and patiently, and many times with a lot of laughter.

Imagine that each experience within each role in your life was and/or is a party you have decided to attend – you had a mindset of joining a party, it was your decision – whether you were aware of it, or not. Consequently, you may also choose to 'leave' the party – ceasing to take part in that that you deem unhealthy for you.

I would like to quote two wisdom pearls from Leonardo Da Vinci that could help you:

"Wisdom is the daughter of experience", and

"Take nothing for granted."

Go ahead, and unfold your life *courageously*.

A Thought Put To Paper

The best way to start the 'party' investigation is to start at the beginning.

You are a Human Being, but you do have some prescribed definitions from the outset – your birth.

Were you born Female or Male?

Single birth, or twins, identical or not?

Healthy or Handicapped?

Single child, or with siblings?

To a single parent family, or of two?

Wealthy or poor circumstances?

Easy birth, or with complications?

What is your constitution type? (You may, for example, consult Ayur Veda to find out.)

Etc.

Please list, for yourself, things that were materially prescribed at your birth time.

Actors, Audience, and The Stage

A Thought Put To Paper

What would you deem could be the initial roles you have played as a baby? This question could be a tricky one, as at times our existence was yearned for, and at others, unwanted.

Our parents might have celebrated us, or regretted us.

It is important to continue being in a party mindset, and relate to it all just as an experience for gaining wisdom versus a soap opera.

At the same time, those first emotional, and behavioural, impressions did dictate (to a degree) our upcoming choices, roles, and experiences.

Obtain an analytical view, and list the particulars without engaging in emotionally charged outlook. That said, you may acknowledge the feelings evoked by this exercise, and by the memories that come up, and let them go.

Actors, Audience, and The Stage

A Thought Put To Paper

When looking at your birth time, there are number of influences that could have affected you, whether you believe in them, or not.

Your physical appearance could either have been received naturally, or was questioned, for instance, a brown eyed child born to parents both having blue eyes; Needless to say that this is a mild example, but you get my drift.

Even your Astrological sign and ascended might have equipped you with certain traits. I always say that those traits might be vices, or virtues, and while the virtues can remain as they are, it is of a benefit to transform the vices to virtues, by learning the lessons they present quickly.

List all these particulars for you to be able to use as signposts later.

Actors, Audience, and The Stage

A Thought Put To Paper

We should make a pause here, and turn our attention to the different environments that you were born to; they all affected you in a way.

A short list of environments would be:
- Physical;
- Religious;
- Relational – in the family;
- Relational – in society;
- Economical;
- A time of peace, or war;
- Country;
- Culture;
- Weather;
- Sexual;

… and more.

Believe it or not, people do behave differently in hot, or cold, weather. If you are a woman, or a man, country, and culture will have something to say too.

Please Enhance the list, as needed.

Actors, Audience, and The Stage

A Thought Put To Paper

In you PHYSICAL environment there were things that affected you directly. An example would be a true story of one native Amazonian that was taken out of the Amazon forest, and brought to the seashore. He reacted with great fear and confusion, because he never had such a vast outlook of distance and horizon, he only knew the very closeness of the jungle trees, with hardly any great size of skies to look at.

List the attributes of your physical environment, both outside and inside your dwellings. Be encouraged to ask yourself if any of the attributes inspired you towards freedom, seclusion, loneliness, sharing, celebration, adventurism, need for privacy, and more.

I am sure you can see that a desert dweller will look at life differently than a mountain dweller, etc.

Apropos, your constitution type will actually be helped, or aggravated by your physical surroundings.

Actors, Audience, and The Stage

A Thought Put To Paper

In your RELIGIOUS environment you may also had many things that affected you. I know it might be impolite to speak about religion, but let us look at it in general terms.

For instance, the same person could have been born to an extreme orthodox religious family, or reformed, or even atheist – I am quite sure that you could see the differences that will apply to that person, in each instance, and particularly, if the person was born male or female.

Even the basic belief or lack thereof, in a greater force, divine deity, God, Creator, All-That-Is, or any other name given to it, will affect the person thinking, behaviour, and experiences.

Even specific types of understandings of religious scriptures, or dogmas, may inflict either sufferings, or celebration, to the infant, child, or adult.

'For your eyes only' list what do you think made a difference in your life, in this religious regard.

You might need to meditate upon this point – more than once.

A Thought Put To Paper

In Family Relational particulars, your position in the family, even the order and ages of siblings, anything from eldest child parenting syndrome to youngest child extreme dealings from celebration to abuse.

Did you have to be a surrogate mother to your younger sibling(s), or were you suffering the myriad 'inconveniences' of the youngest child.

In addition:

Was your family large, or small?

Living in one place, or moving around? It does make a difference on family relations.

Having a homemaker parent, or being babysat more often?

Please add more attributes that you feel makes a difference.

Actors, Audience, and The Stage

A Thought Put To Paper

In Society Relational particulars, a lot may depend on people's belief systems regarding:

Class;

Race;

Gender;

Education level;

Neighbourhood position;

Occupation;

Profession;

…and so much more.

It seems that people like to 'categorise' others, so they will be able to automate their patterns of behaviour, instead of adapting with compassion and appreciation towards all.

Actors, Audience, and The Stage

A Thought Put To Paper

Economic Environment is actually a carryon from the Society Relational particulars, and many times goes hand-in-hand with it.

The differences of circumstances will be the first in line to define the affects put on your life, and then the particular family situation.

For example, in the previous centuries, an aristocratic orphan enjoyed a vastly different opportunities in life, to that of a poor orphan, assuming the poor one would even have lived to see a life longer than a few years.

In the twentieth century, we had many stories of poor people successfully leaving their poor circumstances, and reaching great heights in society.

Yet, if you happened to be born at a recession time, in your country or even globally, you would not have had the magnificent education of what abundance is unless, taught specifically; Undoubtedly, this will affect your outlook in life.

Therefore, list all economical, and financial in particular, circumstances at your birth, and childhood.

Actors, Audience, and The Stage

A Thought Put To Paper

Living in a time of peace, or war plays heavily on what I call 'the equilibrium pendulum' of your life.

At a wartime, you do not feel secured, and are faced with so many unknowns that result in overwhelm. It is not only your own feelings that play havoc on your equilibrium, but also those of your immediate family, and society at large.

At peacetime, you easily take things for granted, so much so that if war explodes in your country, a great shock might follow.

It is the ratio of balance and harmony that denotes how your emotional pendulum will react. Thus, to be reactive is a natural expression although, learning to be pro-active is the redeeming quality of wisdom.

The other factor is 'who is more important?' At peacetime, you have more individual – personal attention, and at wartime, you are to put yourself aside – for the greater good.

In addition, your country, or society, may experience multiple wars during your lifetime.

Actors, Audience, and The Stage

A Thought Put To Paper

The country you live in is a special environment built from the individual to the collective.

A country has an identified personality that may be observed quite easily, and in turn, affects its residents. Could you imagine a tardy person being successful in a country that values punctuality?

The country's identity spills over to every facet of life in it.

Laid-back versus volatile and hot-tempered, graceful and poised versus aggressive, domineering versus collaborative, sport oriented versus lazy, and many more comparisons as such.

The country's picture will be coloured by many things including, terrain, main religion (if any), natural resources, riches, position in the world, island versus continent, all of this will affect its people, and be affected by them, in turn.

Ask yourself, how did your country affected you where, maybe another country would have not.

A Thought Put To Paper

You belong to the culture you were born to, willingly, or not. At infancy, you have to deal with what is given, and only when you grow up you may make changes – and only to the degree, that survival dictates.

Culture is made by a number of factors, some we already touched upon like, religion, physical environment, race, and so on.

The country identity, I spoke of previously, also affects the culture, but in one country, you might have multiple cultures.

Culture dictates patterns of thought, behaviour, belief systems, customs, and expectations – just to mention a few.

Like any other system, a culture has good and bad points. It is wise to decipher those points, which are beneficial for your highest good, and see if you can, or have to, accommodate the rest.

Remember that a culture is not a prison, it is a gift for you to value. If you find that your culture restricts you to the point of despair, you will have to make some different choices.

A Thought Put To Paper

The weather in your immediate environment, in reality, can determine whether you would live, or die, suffer, or enjoy your life.

There are extremes, like the multiple tsunami that hit Japan, and all the devastation they cause. Rogue waves were spoken of for many centuries, and how they wiped off all living in their wake.

People live differently in ice-age periods to the kind of weather types we have today.

In Canada, we fondly call the people who prefer a warmer weather – 'Snow Birds', because the practically leave the county for the duration of the winter months.

Your physical constitution, tendency to allergies, and other personal traits, will set you apart even from your family members.

Choose Life, and find the place for your optimal health in the world.

Can you identify how the weather in your environment affects you?

Actors, Audience, and The Stage

A Thought Put To Paper

Oh Dear! We are now to touch (only lightly) upon your Sexual Environment.

I would like to be clear that we do not deal here with personal sexual history, consented or abusive. We are to look at the patterns of belief, and behaviours, common in your environment.

We all heard stories of exceptions, but it is the norm, that has to be looked at, here. In this subject, religion, culture, and historical habits played a major role.

Take for example the 1960s, it was called the sex revolution, and everything from miniskirts to nudism, drugs, and free sex was tried on.

I would like to ask you to look at your society, from the small circle of your own family, to a greater circle of your friends, to even a greater circle of your culture, religion, and country. Try to understand what are the sexual values of each, and how did they affect your conscious and non-conscious choices, and experiences, you made in life. Remember:

"Wisdom is the daughter of experience."

Actors, Audience, and The Stage

A Thought Put To Paper

The reason we took the pause to look at the greater environment is that when coming back to you, now, will make it easier for you to distinguish what is yours, and what is not.

Although, I always say that we chose everything pertaining to our lives, including where we were born to, I certainly acknowledge that the degree, to which things have transpired, was not chosen for, but the hand we were dealt with, beyond our choice.

Easier illustration would be to watch yourself when you get angry, and acknowledge the many degrees, from being slightly displeased, to being totally livid. In the same way, the people in your life might have amplified their behaviour to more than you could have envisaged.

Henceforth, in a very methodical and patient manner, try to identify what is it that you consciously brought into your life, and what has come to you from the myriad influences talked of in the previous pages. This is not a game of laying the blame at someone's feet, but an exercise in identifying what is, within your control, to change.

Actors, Audience, and The Stage

A Thought Put To Paper

To your aid, and very sincere at that, come your physical body.

Each and every cell your body comprises is conscious; Each holds wisdom beyond what you may imagine, and also has access to the Universal Wisdom.

Your body sends you signals continuously, better even than the traffic signposts that may help you to drive more safely.

To start, any minute headache, dizziness, coughing, itching, and or breathing difficulty is an immediate 'pay attention' call; This call, may originate from your physical body, but may also be triggered by your emotional body, or your mind.

You may feel that things seem to feel surreal – while the cause in surrealism may be either positive, or negative, it is still something that the whole of you is not adjusting to with ease.

By becoming more, or even continuously, of an observer – audience, you could *'stand on guard'* for your own being, and all parts of you will readily cooperate.

Actors, Audience, and The Stage

A Thought Put To Paper

While watching your own bodily and conceptual sensations, ask yourself if the experience, you are in the midst of, has been originated by you, or another.

Firstly, trust yourself, and make peace with your body. Remember that your whole body is conscious, and built of numerous consciousnesses.

Therefore, trust your body.

A funny anecdote is an experience of a sensitive person put into an environment of great noise, e.g., a disco. While many people enjoy loud and fast music, some become ill from it. Now ask, where is the problem originated from, and you will see that it is the coming together of a non-agreeable parts that is the cause. This is how allergies are created.

Kinesiology is a whole science that was developed in order to deepen the understanding between body and mind, and is a very good tool to help distinguish your own messaging to yourself.

Even a thorough washing of the hands may help to relieve an unknown cause of uneasiness.

Actors, Audience, and The Stage

A Thought Put To Paper

An important question for you to ask yourself is whether you are *'aware'* of the life you live in.

Many will be credulous to discover that what they thought their life was – is not actually.

I am sure you are familiar with the term of 'being on an autopilot', ask yourself then, are you on an autopilot mode in any aspect of your life?

Being aware of what you do in life means that you made a conscious choice to perform that specific activity. This is the reason behind the distinction between choice and Right Choice, guess and Educated Guess, consensual or forced.

It is actually quite easy to distinguish if you take the first step to be fully in the present moment, and not have a divided mind scattering to other times – past or future.

You may also ask yourself if you want to perform this activity – you might find it more enjoyable if you do, or get out of it if you do not.

Take full charge of YOU.

A Thought Put To Paper

Life is living in a reality as per the theme of your life, including the plays you engaged yourself with.

Being *Authentically You,* means that you are true to the *Life-Theme* you have chosen, and any diversion from it has to have a justifiable reason.

Therefore, investigate what is 'correct' for your 'theme', and what might be an illusion, or phantom.

Society might have created a belief system in you that dictates that you will behave, or do, certain things, but it might just turn out to be an illusion. A very good example is what happened in England during the WWII whereby, the men left to fight, and the women needed to go and work at the factories, and many other jobs men used to perform during peacetime.

Be easy with yourself, and never beat yourself up for anything. Life is a series of experiences, and you are just weaving your way through them.

Be just, and try your best.

Actors, Audience, and The Stage

A Thought Put To Paper

Just as a reminder, please take into consideration that you are a complex being, nothing is measured in black and white – all is numerous shades of gray in between the black and white.

I see the conglomeration of your consciousness similar in form to an Iceberg, because it is One. Yes, parts are seen, and most of it is unseen, but all is conscious.

Sometimes, your unseen part will nudge you, and your seen part will participate, and sometimes not.

Some good questions to ask when you feel pressured is:

What play do I take part in now?

Did I choose to be part of it?

Did I play this role before?

Am I repeating myself needlessly?

Am I in a position to choose differently?

Take your time and be kind to yourself.

Actors, Audience, and The Stage

Actors, Audience, and The Stage

Actors, Audience, and The Stage

A word about this series

In this busy day and age, where people have more input than they sometimes able to concentrate on, I venture to offer a more succinct manner of dealing with subjects of interest, or need.

The image of a tip of an iceberg immediately brings to mind that there is much more unseen, underwater if you may.

Consciousness is very much like the waters of a vast sea whereby, our conscious thoughts are those that exist above the water level, and our submerged portion of the conscious – is very much our unknown part therefore, many times, it is called the sub-conscious, or the unconscious.

Our feelings are just the waves, and wave crests, which are created by the winds of time, and occurrences of life upon the surface.

I would like to have your brief time of contemplation in reading this short book yet, to impress your mind with a profound message, and content.

It is in the succinct that we may never be overwhelmed, and in overpowering vast amount of input that we are fatigued.

I trust you know that much more could have been said about the subject of the book, but maybe what was said is enough.

I wish you joy and peace – always.

www.ingramcontent.com/pod-product-compliance
Lightning Source LLC
Chambersburg PA
CBHW020902020526
44112CB00052B/1197